Alabama

BY ANN HEINRICHS

Content Adviser: J. Steven Murray, Managing Editor, *The Alabama Review,*
Auburn University, Auburn, Alabama

Reading Adviser: Dr. Linda D. Labbo, Department of Reading Education,
College of Education, The University of Georgia

Gainesboro Elementary School
Winchester, Virginia

COMPASS POINT BOOKS MINNEAPOLIS, MINNESOTA

Compass Point Books
3109 West 50th Street, #115
Minneapolis, MN 55410

Visit Compass Point Books on the Internet at *www.compasspointbooks.com*
or e-mail your request to *custserv@compasspointbooks.com*

On the cover: State capitol in Montgomery

Photographs ©: Unicorn Stock Photos/Andre Jenny, cover, 1; Courtesy of Mobile Area Convention and Visitors Bureau, 3, 6, 11, 28, 30, 39, 41, 47, 48 (top); Photo Network/Dennis MacDonald, 5; Unicorn Stock Photos/Kelly Parris, 7; Corbis/William A. Blake, 8; Index Stock Imagery/Jeff Greenberg, 10; Hulton/Archive by Getty Images, 12, 14, 15, 16, 17, 32, 33; Alabama Archives, 13; Corbis/Peter Yates, 18; Unicorn Stock Photos/Dennis MacDonald, 19, 43 (top); John Elk III, 20, 22, 36, 38, 40, 42, 45; U.S. Department of Agriculture/Don Schuhart, 23; Courtesy of Dr. Roger Lien, Auburn University Poultry Science Department, 24; Corbis/Kelly/Mooney Photography, 25; John Sohlden/Visuals Unlimited, 26; Unicorn Stock Photos/Jeff Greenberg, 27; Stock Montage, 29, 46; Photo Network/Nancy Hoyt Belcher, 31; Jeff Greenberg/Visuals Unlimited, 34; Courtesy of McWane Center/Jim Little, 37; Robesus, Inc., 43 (state flag); One Mile Up, Inc., 43 (state seal); Mack Henley/Visuals Unlimited, 44 (top left); Unicorn Stock Photos/Ted Rose, 44 (bottom left); PhotoDisc, 44 (bottom right).

Editors: E. Russell Primm, Emily J. Dolbear, and Patricia Stockland
Photo Researcher: Marcie C. Spence
Photo Selector: Linda S. Koutris
Designer/Page Production: The Design Lab/Jaime Martens
Cartographer: XNR Productions, Inc.

Library of Congress Cataloging-in-Publication Data
Heinrichs, Ann.
  Alabama / by Ann Heinrichs.
     p. cm.— (This land is your land)
Includes bibliographical references and index.
Contents: Welcome to Alabama!—Mountains, coasts, and plains—A trip through time—Government by the people—Alabamians at work—Getting to know Alabamians—Let's explore Alabama!
  ISBN 0-7565-0332-9
  1. Alabama—Juvenile literature. [1. Alabama.] I. Title. II. Series.
  F326.3 .H45 2004
  976.1—dc21   *15837*   2002012860

Table of Contents

NOTE: In this book, words that are defined in the glossary are in **bold** *the first time they appear in the text.*

"When you're working around a blast furnace . . . everything's dangerous—overhead, underhead, dangerous work." Those are the words of Clarence Dean. Day after day, he labored at blazing furnaces of **molten iron.**

Clarence worked at Sloss Furnaces in Birmingham, Alabama. The furnaces melted iron ore to remove wastes. Their smokestacks belched black clouds into the skies. Cotton had once been "king" in Alabama, but iron and steel took its place.

Today, Alabama is a leading farm and factory state. Montgomery is the state capital. This city played an important role in the history of the South. It was the first capital of the Confederate States of America. These Southern states fought the Union in the Civil War (1861–1865). The civil rights movement was born in Montgomery, too. Dr. Martin Luther King Jr. organized his first protests there.

Alabama is also a popular place for visitors. They love its forests, lakes, beaches, and historic sites. You will, too!

▲ Bellingrath Gardens in Theodore

Mountains, Coasts, and Plains

▲ **The skyline along Mobile Bay**

Alabama is one of the nation's southern states. Mississippi lies to its west, and Georgia is on its east. To the north is Tennessee. South of Alabama are Florida and the Gulf of Mexico.

Only a small piece of southwestern Alabama reaches the Gulf. Alabama is lucky to have this stretch of coast. It gives the state a way to ship goods to faraway ports. Mobile Bay cuts inland from the Gulf. The Mobile and Alabama Rivers flow into it. At the head of the bay is Mobile, a seaport city. Dauphin Island sits at the mouth of the bay.

Northeast Alabama is hilly. Lush forests cover its rolling hills. Rivers and streams cut valleys into the hillsides. Here and there, the rivers splash down in sparkling waterfalls. The Tennessee River cuts across northern Alabama. Its many dams create huge lakes.

▲ **One of many creeks running through Marshall County**

▲ Cheaha Mountain, Alabama's highest point, is located in the foothills of the Appalachians.

Three high geographic regions dominate northern Alabama. They are the Piedmont, the Appalachian Ridge and Valley, and the Cumberland Plateau. The Piedmont is in the east. It's rich in coal, iron, limestone, and marble. North of the Piedmont range is the Appalachian Ridge and Valley. It, too, contains rich mineral deposits. Birmingham, Alabama's largest city, is in this region. Farther northwest is the Cumberland Plateau. This land is lower and flatter. Its major city is Huntsville.

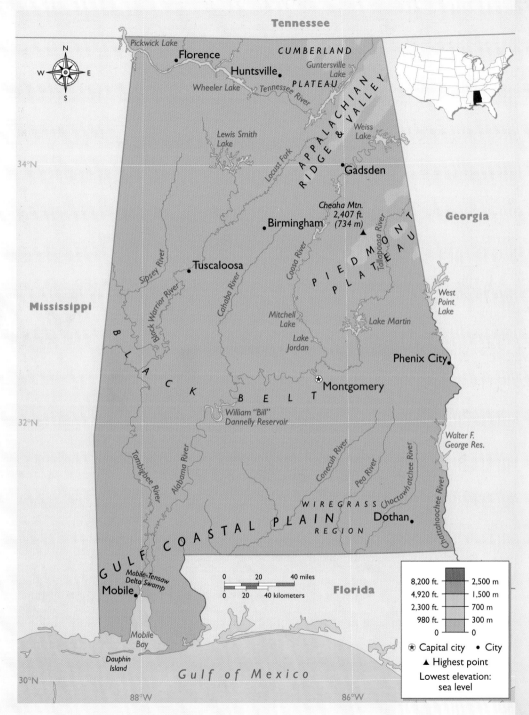

Tennessee

Pickwick Lake
Florence
Huntsville
CUMBERLAND
Guntersville
Lake
PLATEAU
Wheeler Lake
Tennessee River

Lewis Smith
Lake
APPALACHIAN
RIDGE & VALLEY
Weiss
Lake

Locust Fork

34°N
Gadsden

Cheaha Mtn.
2,407 ft.
(734 m)
Birmingham
▲
Georgia

Coosa River
Tallapoosa River
PIEDMONT
PLATEAU

Sipsey River
Tuscaloosa
Cahaba River

West
Point
Lake

Black Warrior River
Mississippi
Mitchell
Lake
Lake Martin

B
Lake
Jordan

L

A

C
Phenix City

K
William "Bill"
Dannelly Reservoir
Montgomery

B E L T

32°N
Walter F.
George Res.

Tombigbee River
Alabama River
Conecuh River
Pea River
Choctawhatchee River

Chattahoochee River

WIREGRASS
Dothan
REGION

G
U
L
F
C
O
A
S
T
A
L
P
L
A
I
N

Mobile-Tensaw
Delta Swamp
Mobile
Florida

| 0 | 20 | 40 miles |
| 0 | 20 | 40 kilometers |

Mobile
Bay

Dauphin
Island
Gulf of Mexico

30°N

88°W
86°W

8,200 ft.	2,500 m
4,920 ft.	1,500 m
2,300 ft.	700 m
980 ft.	300 m
0	0

⊛ Capital city • City
▲ Highest point
Lowest elevation:
sea level

▲ **A topographic map of Alabama**

The Gulf Coastal Plain covers most of southern Alabama. Its northern section is covered with pine forests. Toward the west, the soil is full of sand and gravel and not very fertile. The southwest section, around Mobile Bay, is swampy. The southeast is called the Wiregrass region. It is named for the wiry grass that used to grow there. Now this is a fertile farming region.

The Black Belt cuts across the middle of the Coastal Plain. It has rich, dark soil. This strip of land curves around like a big smile. It runs all the way from the western border with Mississippi to the eastern border with Georgia.

▲ **Sunset on Mobile Bay at Fairhope**

▲ Alabama's beaches are popular places during the summer.

Forests cover more than half the state. They're home to deer, foxes, raccoons, and bobcats. Beavers build their homes in the rivers and swamps. Alligators lurk in the swamps, too. Crabs, shrimp, oysters, and many fish live off the coast.

Alabamians enjoy mild weather. Winters do not usually get very cold, although most of the state gets at least some snow or ice each year. The far south gets the most rain. Summers are warm. Then people head for the sunny beaches along the coast or to the cooler mountains in the north.

People were living in Alabama thousands of years ago. Cliff dwellers lived in the caves of northern Alabama. Mound builders lived near Tuscaloosa. They buried their dead in large earthen mounds. Later, many Native American groups settled in Alabama. They included Cherokee, Chickasaw, Choctaw, and Creek people. They raised corn, beans, squash, and tobacco.

Spanish explorers were the first Europeans in Alabama. Alonso Álvarez de Piñeda sailed into Mobile Bay in 1519. Hernando de Soto marched through in 1540. A chief named Tuscaloosa invited de Soto to Mabila, a large village located somewhere along the Alabama River. There a fierce battle broke out, and hundreds of Native Americans were killed.

▲ Spanish explorer Hernando de Soto

▲ **The French founded Fort Louis in 1702.**

In 1702, the French founded Fort Louis on the Mobile River. It was the capital of France's vast Louisiana colony. The fort was moved to the site of present-day Mobile in 1711. Mobile passed to Great Britain and then to Spain. The United States gained northern Alabama in 1795. It finally won Mobile in the War of 1812 (1812–1815).

Meanwhile, settlers kept pushing into Native American lands. The Creeks fought hard to hold onto their territory but were defeated in the Battle of Horseshoe Bend in 1814.

In 1819, Alabama became the twenty-second state. Settlers raised cotton on huge farms called plantations. Thousands of Africans were forced to work the farms as slaves. Soon, the U.S. government began taking steps to outlaw slavery. However, most white Alabamians believed that the control of slavery should be left for each state to decide. Alabama and other southern states seceded, or separated, from the Union. They formed the Confederate States of America, and its capital was Montgomery. Soon the Civil War broke out. The Confederacy lost the war in 1865, and all slaves were freed.

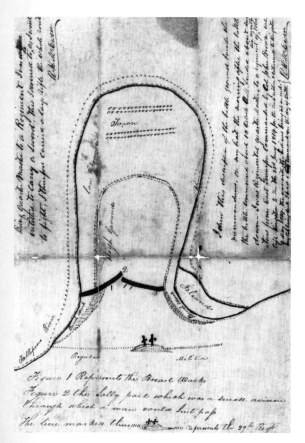

▲ A map of Horseshoe Bend from 1814, the same year the Americans defeated the Creek Indians in Alabama

▲ Sharecroppers picking cotton

After the war, many former slaves and poor whites worked as sharecroppers. That means they paid a share of their crops as rent. New industries began to spring up, too. Coal and iron were found in north-central Alabama near the mountains, so businessmen created Birmingham. The city soon had booming iron and steel mills. Textile mills that produced clothes and linens of all types appeared in other areas of the state.

The 1920s and 1930s brought hard times to Alabama. Cotton pests and **soil erosion** ruined many farms. Then the nation's Great Depression struck. Thousands of Alabamians lost their homes, farms, and jobs.

The U.S. government created the Tennessee Valley Authority (TVA) in 1933. The TVA built dams along the Tennessee River. The dams controlled flooding and provided water-powered electricity. Because of this, many Alabamians got electricity and running water for the first time. During World War II (1939–1945), Huntsville's Redstone **Arsenal** made war supplies. Alabama built ships and trained troops and pilots, too.

▲ During World War II, Alabamians manufactured war supplies like this missile.

▲ **Martin Luther King Jr. played an important role in Alabama's civil rights history.**

Race relations had been poor in Alabama for a long time, but they came to a head in the 1950s and 1960s. In 1955, police in Montgomery arrested a black woman named Rosa Parks. She had refused to give up her bus seat to a white person. Civil rights leader Martin Luther King Jr. organized a bus **boycott.** Blacks in Montgomery stopped riding buses until the city agreed to treat white and black passengers as equals. Later, King led many civil rights marches. Slowly, blacks gained protection of their rights as citizens.

▲ A worker in the training center at the Mercedes Benz automobile plant in Tuscaloosa

Today, Alabama's farms and factories are different but still very busy. Cotton plantations have been replaced by poultry and cattle farms. Less steel is produced now, but Alabama has several factories that build automobiles. Many more Alabamians work in offices, shops, and schools. The TVA projects that brought electricity to much of the state also created many lakes and recreation areas. These are still enjoyed by both residents and visitors.

Government by the People

▲ **The state capitol in Montgomery**

Montgomery is Alabama's capital city. The state capitol stands on a high hill. It's known as Goat Hill because herds of goats grazed there many years ago. Inside and near the capitol are all the important state government offices.

The design of Alabama's state government is similar to that of the U.S. government. It's divided into three branches. They are called the legislative, executive, and judicial branches. This division creates a good balance of power.

▲ Alabama's state senators meet in this chamber in Montgomery.

The legislative branch makes the state laws. It also decides how the state will spend its money. Alabama's lawmakers serve in the state legislature. It has two houses, or parts. One is the 35-member senate. The other is the 105-member house of representatives. Each lawmaker represents the people who live in his or her **district.** Voters in those districts choose their lawmakers.

The executive branch's job is to enforce the law. That means making sure the laws are obeyed. Alabama's governor is the head of the executive branch. Voters elect a governor every four

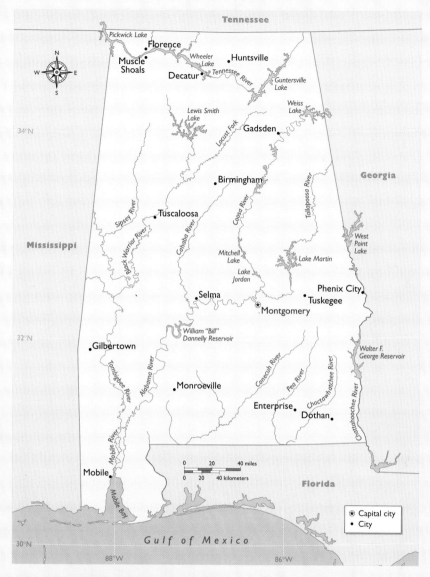

▲ **A geopolitical map of Alabama**

years. The governor can serve any number of terms. However,

he or she can serve only twice in a row. Voters also elect several

other executive officers.

The judicial branch is made up of judges. They hear the cases of people or groups who disagree or have broken the law. Alabama's highest court is the state supreme court. Voters elect its nine justices, or judges, for a six-year term.

Alabama is divided into sixty-seven counties. Voters in each county elect county commissioners. The probate judge is the head commissioner in most counties. Other county officers include the sheriff and the district attorney. Most cities and towns elect a city council that makes local laws. They also elect a mayor to serve as the community's chief executive.

▲ Judges in Mobile decide cases in City Hall.

▲ **An Alabama peanut harvest**

"King Cotton" was once the center of Alabama's economy, but insects called **boll weevils** swept through in 1915. They wiped out the cotton crops. Now Alabamians say that disaster was also a blessing. It forced farmers to raise other crops.

Cotton is still Alabama's top crop, though. Most of it grows in the Tennessee River Valley in the northern part of the state. Farmers also grow corn, soybeans, peanuts, wheat, and other crops. Alabama ranks fourth in the nation in peanuts. It ranks fifth in sweet potatoes and pecans. However, chickens bring in the most farm income. Alabama ranks third in the country in broilers. Those are chickens that are five to twelve weeks old. Alabama is also a great state for catfish. It produces more catfish than any other state except Mississippi.

▲ Poultry farms, like this one at the Auburn University Poultry Science Department, have replaced some of Alabama's cotton plantations.

▲ **Paper is one of Alabama's top products.**

Today, manufacturing is Alabama's leading industry. The most valuable factory goods are fertilizer, paint, and artificial fibers. Paper and wood pulp are top products, too. They come from Alabama's abundant forests. Steelmaking is another important industry. Steel mills operate in Birmingham, Decatur, and Gadsden.

Natural gas is Alabama's leading mineral product. Many of the gas regions also contain petroleum, or oil. Alabama's coal is important in the steel industry. Other valuable minerals are limestone, cement, crushed stone, and clays.

Gainesboro Elementary School
Winchester, Virginia

Most of Alabama's workers sell services. They're likely to find jobs in the bigger cities. Engineers and computer programmers are service workers. Many work at Marshall Space Flight Center in Huntsville. Health care workers, bankers, and teachers are all service workers, too. So are people in Alabama's wholesale trades. Wholesalers buy large amounts of farm, factory, and mining products. Then they sell these goods to various companies.

In spite of its industries, Alabama has many poor people. Alabama's poverty

▲ **Rockets at the Marshall Space Flight Center**

▲ **The Southern Poverty Law Center is in Montgomery. Its office is the site of the Civil Rights Memorial, which honors those who died during the civil rights movement.**

level is very high. Many Alabamians are unemployed, too. Black residents suffer the most from poverty and unemployment. The state is working hard to make life better for all its people.

Getting to Know Alabamians

▲ The Mobile Convention Center is located in Mobile, Alabama's third-largest city.

In 2000, there were 4,447,100 people in Alabama. That made it twenty-third in population among the states. Birmingham is the largest city. It's a major manufacturing center. Next in size is Montgomery. Mobile, the third-largest city, is a seaport with many historic sites. Huntsville is a center for Alabama's space industry.

Alabama has a larger African-American population than most states. About one of every four Alabamians is black. Most live in the larger cities and in southern Alabama. A small number of Alabamians are **Hispanic,** Asian, or Native American. Not many people are foreign born, though. Most of Alabama's white people are descendants of early settlers. They may have roots in Ireland, England, or Germany.

Many music **traditions** are alive in Alabama. They include jazz, blues, gospel, and country music. Muscle Shoals is known for its many recording studios. Alabamian W. C. Handy is called the "Father of the Blues." He wrote "Saint Louis Blues" and many other classic tunes. Banjo and fiddle music are long-time folk traditions. Quilt and pottery making are Alabama folk arts, too.

▲ *"Father of the Blues" W. C. Handy*

▲ This dragon float is part of Mobile's Mardi Gras festivities.

Mobile's Mardi Gras is a very large event. This weeklong carnival is held in February or March. People parade through the streets in fantastic costumes. Mobile also holds an azalea festival and hosts the Junior Miss Pageant. Birmingham presents a rose festival and a spring arts festival. Every May, Monroeville hosts a stage production of *To Kill a Mockingbird*. Monroeville native Harper Lee wrote the book. This dramatic tale explores racial prejudice in the South. The book was made into a movie in 1962.

Booker T. Washington founded Tuskegee Institute in 1881. Washington had been born a slave. He opened the institute to teach African-Americans skills for success. Today, the institute is called Tuskegee University and remains well known for its programs in agriculture, engineering, and veterinary medicine.

▲ **Carnegie Hall on the campus of Tuskegee University**

Football season is an exciting time in Alabama. People take sides to root for their favorite college team. Half the state is wild about the Auburn University Tigers. The other half cheers for the University of Alabama's Crimson Tide.

Many great athletes have come from Alabama. They include boxer Joe Louis and Olympic track star Jesse Owens. Football great Joe Namath is an Alabamian. Basketball champ

▲ **A 2000 game between the Auburn Tigers and the Alabama Crimson Tide**

▲ Willie Mays, the "Say Hey Kid," played baseball for the New York Giants, the San Francisco Giants, and the New York Mets. He was elected to the National Baseball Hall of Fame in 1979.

Charles Barkley came from Alabama, too. So did baseball stars Hank Aaron, Satchel Paige, and Willie Mays. Bo Jackson was a football and baseball star.

▲ The Sequoyah Caverns are located in Valley Head.

Do you like to go spelunking? That means exploring caves. If you do, then Alabama's the place for you. Prehistoric cave dwellers once lived in DeSoto **Caverns.** Now you can tour these awesome underground caves. Sequoyah Caverns and Cathedral Caverns are great for spelunkers, too.

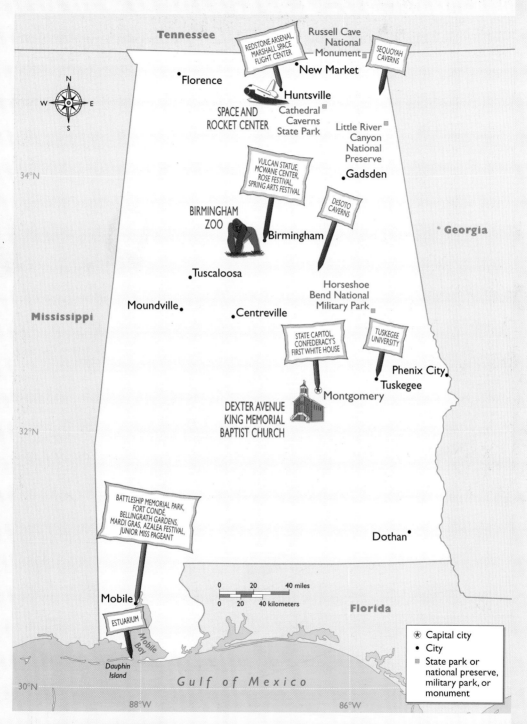

Tennessee

Russell Cave National Monument

REDSTONE ARSENAL, MARSHALL SPACE FLIGHT CENTER

SEQUOYAH CAVERNS

• Florence

• New Market

Huntsville

SPACE AND ROCKET CENTER

Cathedral Caverns State Park

Little River Canyon National Preserve

VULCAN STATUE, MCWANE CENTER, ROSE FESTIVAL, SPRING ARTS FESTIVAL

• Gadsden

BIRMINGHAM ZOO

DESOTO CAVERNS

Birmingham

Georgia

• Tuscaloosa

Moundville •

Horseshoe Bend National Military Park

• Centreville

STATE CAPITOL, CONFEDERACY'S FIRST WHITE HOUSE

TUSKEGEE UNIVERSITY

Phenix City •

Tuskegee

Montgomery

DEXTER AVENUE KING MEMORIAL BAPTIST CHURCH

Mississippi

BATTLESHIP MEMORIAL PARK, FORT CONDÉ, BELLINGRATH GARDENS, MARDI GRAS, AZALEA FESTIVAL, JUNIOR MISS PAGEANT

Dothan •

0   20   40 miles
0   20   40 kilometers

Florida

Mobile

ESTUARIUM

Mobile Bay

Dauphin Island

Gulf of Mexico

34°N

32°N

30°N

88°W

86°W

★ Capital city
• City
▪ State park or national preserve, military park, or monument

▲ Places to visit in Alabama

Alabama's earliest known people lived in Russell Cave. You can see their tools and pottery in the museum there. Nearby is scenic Little River Canyon. It's the deepest canyon in the eastern United States. Moundville is another prehistoric site. More than forty Native American mounds remain there.

▲ Little River Falls is part of Little River Canyon National Preserve.

▲ **An ocean exhibit at the McWane Center**

A huge statue of Vulcan looks over Birmingham. Vulcan was the ancient Romans' god of fire and metalworking. He represents the city's iron and steel industry. At Birmingham Zoo, you can feed the lorikeets. These Australian parrots are well trained. They land on your arm and sip from your cup! Birmingham's McWane Center is a hands-on science museum. There you'll explore dinosaurs, planets, electricity, and much more.

Climb into your space capsule. You're ready for astronaut training! That's what awaits you at Huntsville's Space and Rocket Center. You'll also see a huge collection of rockets and other spacecraft. The center holds weeklong Space Camps, too.

In Montgomery, you can tour the state capitol. The Confederacy's first White House is in Montgomery, too. Confederate president Jefferson Davis lived there. Dexter Avenue King Memorial Baptist Church is an important civil rights landmark. Dr. Martin Luther King Jr. was the pastor there from September 1954 to November 1959.

Want to take your place at the controls of a battleship or a submarine? Just head down to Battleship Memorial Park on Mobile Bay. There you'll find the battleship USS *Alabama*. It served in World War II. The submarine USS *Drum* did, too. Visitors can climb all over them!

▲ Dr. Martin Luther King Jr. was pastor of the Dexter Avenue King Memorial Baptist Church.

▲ Fort Condé is designed to look like an eighteenth-century French fort.

Fort Condé is rebuilt like a French fort from the 1700s. Costumed "soldiers" fire muskets and cannons. It is all part of Mobile's Welcome Center. From there, you can visit historic homes or Bellingrath Gardens. You can enjoy the water, too!

▲ **A view of Fort Gaines on Dauphin Island**

Ride a riverboat up the Mobile River. Then check out the alligators in the Mobile-Tensaw **Delta** Swamp. On Dauphin Island, you can gather seashells along the beach. The island's Estuarium is like an educational zoo. It's full of sea and swamp animals. Want to see what they feel like? Just reach in the "touch tanks."

Nature thrives here, and history comes to life. Your discovery of Alabama's wonders has just begun!

Important Dates

1519 Alonso Álvarez de Piñeda sails into Mobile Bay.

1540 Hernando de Soto explores Alabama.

1711 The French-Canadian Fort Louis colony moves to the site of present-day Mobile.

1763 France gives Alabama to Great Britain.

1783 Much of Alabama passes from Great Britain to the United States.

1817 Alabama Territory is created.

1819 Alabama becomes the twenty-second state on December 14.

1861 Alabama secedes from the Union and joins the Confederacy.

1868 Alabama rejoins the Union.

1933 The Tennessee Valley Authority (TVA) is created.

1940s The Redstone Arsenal opens in Huntsville.

1944 Oil is discovered in Gilbertown.

1955 Rosa Parks is arrested for not giving up her bus seat to a white passenger; Montgomery's bus boycott begins.

1956 Montgomery is ordered to integrate its public buses.

1960 The George C. Marshall Space Flight Center opens in Huntsville.

1965 The Reverend Martin Luther King Jr. leads a protest march from Selma to Montgomery; it leads to the Voting Rights Act of 1965.

1974 George Wallace becomes Alabama's first governor elected to three terms.

1982 George Wallace becomes Alabama's first governor elected to four terms.

1985 The Tennessee-Tombigbee Waterway opens.

1986 Guy Hunt is elected Alabama's first Republican governor since Reconstruction.

2001 Condoleeza Rice of Birmingham becomes the first woman to be appointed national security adviser.

Glossary

arsenal—a place where guns and ammunition are made or stored

boll weevils—insect pests that feed on cotton plants

boycott—a refusal to buy certain goods or services

caverns—caves

delta—a fertile region near the mouth of a river

district—an area formed by a division of a city for some special purpose, such as electing officials

Hispanic—people of Mexican, South American, and other Spanish-speaking cultures

molten iron—iron melted at a very high temperature

soil erosion—the washing away of fertile topsoil

traditions—customs common among a family or group

Did You Know?

★ Alabama's nickname is the Heart of Dixie. The South is called Dixie—but why? Before the Civil War, a Louisiana bank issued $10 bills. They were printed with the word *dix*. That's French for "ten." As a result, people called the South Dixieland.

★ North America's first Mardi Gras celebration took place in Mobile. *Mardi Gras* is French for "Fat Tuesday." That's the day before Ash Wednesday—the first day of the pre-Easter season of Lent.

★ Huntsville's Marshall Space Flight Center built the first rocket to take humans to the Moon.

★ The city of Mobile is named after the Mauvilla or Mabila Indians.

★ The name "Alabama" may have come from the Choctaw language. It means "those who clear thickets."

★ The Boll Weevil Monument stands in the town of Enterprise. It honors the cotton-eating pest for forcing Alabama's farmers to grow other valuable crops.

★ Montgomery is sometimes called the Cradle of the Confederacy. That's because it was the first capital of the Confederate States of America.

State capital: Montgomery

State motto: *Audemus Jura Nostra Defendere* (Latin for "We Dare Defend Our Rights")

State nickname: Heart of Dixie

Statehood: December 14, 1819; twenty-second state

Land area: 50,750 square miles (131,443 sq km); **rank:** twenty-eighth

Highest point: Cheaha Mountain, 2,407 feet (734 m)

Lowest point: Sea level, along the Gulf of Mexico

Highest recorded temperature: 112°F (44°C) at Centreville on September 5, 1925

Lowest recorded temperature: –27°F (–33°C) at New Market on January 30, 1966

Average January temperature: 46°F (8°C)

Average July temperature: 80°F (27°C)

Population in 2000: 4,447,100; **rank:** twenty-third

Largest cities in 2000: Birmingham (242,820), Montgomery (201,568), Mobile (198,915), Huntsville (158,216)

Factory products: Chemicals, paper products, metals, transportation equipment

Farm products: Chickens, beef cattle, cotton, hogs, peanuts

Mining products: Coal, natural gas, petroleum

State flag: Alabama's state flag may be square or rectangular. It features an X-shaped red cross on a white background. This symbol also appeared on the Confederate flag. The X-shaped cross is also called a Saint Andrew's cross. It recalls the early Christian saint who was crucified on such a cross.

State seal: Alabama's state seal features a map of Alabama showing its major rivers. Alabama's bordering states surround it. Alabama's rivers were important shipping lanes in the state's early days. Today, they are a source of hydroelectric power.

State abbreviations: Ala. (traditional); AL (postal)

State Symbols

State bird: Yellowhammer (flicker)

State flower: Camellia

State tree: Southern longleaf pine

State horse: Racking horse

State game bird: Wild turkey

State saltwater fish: Fighting tarpon

State freshwater fish: Largemouth bass

State reptile: Alabama red-bellied turtle

State amphibian: Red Hills salamander

State insect: Monarch butterfly

State mascot and butterfly: Eastern tiger swallowtail

State wildflower: Oak-leaf hydrangea

State mineral: Hematite (red iron ore)

State rock: Marble

State gemstone: Star blue quartz

State nut: Pecan

State shell: *Scaphella junonia johnstonae* (Johnstone's junonia)

State fossil: *Basilosaurus cetoides* (zeuglodon)

State soil: Bama soil series

State American folk dance: Square dance

Making Pecan Pralines

Pralines are a favorite Southern candy made with pecans!

Makes about a dozen pralines.

INGREDIENTS:

1 cup sugar

1 cup brown sugar, packed

1/2 cup cream or half-and-half

1 1/2 cups pecan halves or pieces

2 teaspoons butter or margarine

DIRECTIONS:

Make sure an adult helps you with the hot stove. Combine sugars and cream in a saucepan. Bring to a boil over medium heat. Stir now and then with a wooden spoon. Cook until it reaches 228°F on a candy thermometer. Add pecan pieces and butter. Keep cooking and stirring. It's done when you can put a drop of the mixture into cold water and it forms a soft ball (about 235°F). Remove from heat and let it cool a few minutes. Then stir until it starts to get thick. Drop big spoonfuls onto waxed paper. Store in a cool, dry place.

State Song

"Alabama"

Words by Julia S. Tutwiler, music by Edna Gockel Gussen

Alabama, Alabama,
We will aye be true to thee,
From thy Southern shore where groweth,
By the sea thine orange tree.
To thy Northern vale where floweth
Deep and blue thy Tennessee.
Alabama, Alabama,
We will aye be true to thee!

Broad the Stream whose name thou bearest;
Grand thy Bigbee rolls along;
Fair thy Coosa-Tallapoosa
Bold thy Warrior, dark and strong.
Goodlier than the land that Moses
Climbed lone Nebo's Mount to see
Alabama, Alabama,
We will aye be true to thee!

From thy prairies broad and fertile,
Where thy snow-white cotton shines,
To the hills where coal and iron
Hide in thy exhaustless mines,
Strong-armed miners—sturdy farmers:
Loyal hearts what'er we be,
Alabama, Alabama,
We will aye be true to thee!

From thy quarries where the marble
White as that of Paros gleams
Waiting till thy sculptor's chisel,
Wake to thy poet's life/dreams;

For not only wealth of nature,
Wealth of mind hast thou to fee.
Alabama, Alabama,
We will aye be true to thee!

Where the perfumed south-wind whispers,
Thy magnolia groves among,
Softer than a mother's kisses,
Sweeter than a mother's song;
Where the golden jasmine trailing,
Woos the treasure-laden bee,
Alabama, Alabama,
We will aye be true to thee!

Brave and pure thy men and women,
Better this than corn and wine,
Make us worthy, God in Heaven,
Of this goodly land of Thine;
Hearts as open as our doorways,
Liberal hands and spirits free,
Alabama, Alabama,
We will aye be true to thee!

Little, little, can I give thee,
Alabama, mother mine;
But that little—hand, brain, spirit,
All I have and am are thine.
Take, O take the gift and giver.
Take and serve thyself with me,
Alabama, Alabama,
I will aye be true to thee.

Hank Aaron (1934–) was a baseball player. He hit a record-breaking 755 home runs in his career. He is director of player development for the Atlanta Braves.

Ralph Abernathy (1926–1990) was a civil rights leader. He helped Dr. Martin Luther King Jr. organize the Montgomery bus boycott in 1955. Later, he was president of the Southern Christian Leadership Conference (SCLC).

Tallulah Bankhead (1903–1968) was an actress. She was known for her elegance and her husky voice.

George Washington Carver (1864–1943) was a botanist, or plant scientist. He headed the plant research department at Tuskegee Institute. Carver developed hundreds of new products from peanuts and sweet potatoes. He was born a slave in Missouri.

Nat "King" Cole (1919–1965) was a popular singer and pianist. He was called "the man with the velvet voice." "Mona Lisa" and "Unforgettable" were two of his hit songs.

W. C. Handy (1873–1958) was a blues songwriter and band leader. Handy (pictured above left) is called the Father of the Blues. His famous tunes include "Saint Louis Blues" and "Beale Street Blues." His initials stand for William Christopher.

Kate Jackson (1948–) is an actress. She first became famous in the television show *Charlie's Angels.*

Helen Keller (1880–1968) was an author and educator who worked for the rights of handicapped people. She lost both her sight and hearing before the age of two.

Coretta Scott King (1927–) is a civil rights leader. Her husband was Dr. Martin Luther King Jr. After he was shot and killed in 1968, she continued his work.

Willie Mays (1931–) played baseball with the New York and San Francisco Giants. He hit 660 home runs during his career.

Jesse Owens (1913–1980) was a champion track-and-field athlete. He broke five world records in one afternoon (May 25, 1935). He won four gold medals in the 1936 Olympic Games.

Rosa Parks (1913–) is a civil rights activist. In 1955, she was arrested for refusing to give up her bus seat to a white passenger. Many consider this to be the beginning of the civil rights movement.

Condoleeza Rice (1954–) is the first woman to serve as U.S. national security adviser. President George W. Bush appointed her in 2001.

George Wallace (1919–1998) was Alabama's governor for a record four terms. At first he was opposed to racial integration. Later, he helped promote it. He was crippled by a gunshot in 1972.

Hank Williams (1923–1953) was a country-western singer. His most famous song is "Cold, Cold Heart."

At the Library

Benjamin, Anne, and Ellen Beier (illustrator). *Young Rosa Parks: Civil Rights Heroine.* Mahwah, N.J.: Troll Associates, 1995.

Brown, Dottie. *Alabama.* Minneapolis: Lerner, 2001.

Feeney, Kathy. *Alabama.* Danbury, Conn.: Children's Press, 2002.

McKissack, Patricia. *Run Away Home.* New York: Scholastic Trade, 1997.

Nobleman, Marc Tyler. *Rosa Parks.* Milwaukee: World Almanac Library, 2002.

Welsbacher, Anne. *Alabama.* Edina, Minn.: Abdo & Daughters, 1998.

On the Web
Welcome to Alabama!

http://www.alabama.gov/
http://www.archives.state.al.us
To learn about Alabama's history, government, economy, and land

Alabama Tourism and Travel

http://www.touralabama.org/index-FL.htm
To find out about Alabama's events, activities, and sights

Through the Mail
Alabama Bureau of Tourism and Travel

401 Adams Avenue, Suite 126
Montgomery, AL 36104
For information on travel and interesting sights in Alabama

Alabama Development Office

401 Adams Avenue, Sixth Floor
Montgomery, AL 36130
For information on Alabama's economy

Office of the Secretary of State

State Capitol
Montgomery, AL 36130
For information about Alabama's government

On the Road
Alabama State House

11 South Union Street
Montgomery, AL 36130
334/242-7800 or 334/242-7600
To visit Alabama's state capitol

Index

About the Author

Ann Heinrichs grew up in Fort Smith, Arkansas, and lives in Chicago. She is the author of more than one hundred books for children and young adults on Asian, African, and U.S. history and culture. Ann has also written numerous newspaper, magazine, and encyclopedia articles. She is an award-winning martial artist, specializing in t'ai chi empty-hand and sword forms.

Ann has traveled widely throughout the United States, Africa, Asia, and the Middle East. In exploring each state for this series, she rediscovered the people, history, and resources that make this a great land, as well as the concerns we share with people around the world.

Gainesboro Elementary School
Winchester, Virginia